SOUTH WEST STEAM

SALISBURY - EXETER - TAUNTON - PENZANCE

1985 to 2008

ROGER SIVITER ARPS

GREAT BEAR PUBLISHING

A reminder of past times as ex SR West Country Pacific No 34027 *Taw Valley* masquerading as No 34045 *Ottery St Mary* reaches the bottom of the 1 in 37 bank from Exeter Central station and approaches Exeter St Davids station with the "Atlantic Coast Express" from Waterloo to Exeter, on 5 September 2004. Note the spire of St Davids church, and also the lines in the foreground, which is the former GWR line from Plymouth.

(Roger Siviter)

Above: The 7 April 1985, after an absence of nearly 20 years, saw the return of main line steam to the south west of England in connection with the GWR 150th anniversary celebrations. The special train was scheduled to run from Bristol to Plymouth, with GWR locomotives King Class 4-6-0 No 6000 *King George V* and Manor Class 4-6-0 No 7819 *Hinton Manor* in charge. However, No 6000 failed at Taunton and was taken off the train and replaced (at the rear of the train) by Class 37 diesel locomotives Nos 37009 and 37178. This combination ran to Exeter St Davids, where No 7819 came off the train, and then the special charter proceeded to Plymouth with the Class 37s in charge.

This picture shows No 7819 (plus the Class 37s) entering Tiverton Junction station on that fateful day where it paused for a "blow-up". Nevertheless, *Hinton Manor* looks a fine sight, surrounded by a splendid array of GWR semaphore signals and much trackwork, most of which would shortly disappear. The truncated line on the right hand side was the start of the Culm Valley line to Hemyock, which closed in 1975.

(Christina Siviter)

Front jacket: On 28 August 2005, GWR King Class 4-6-0 No 6024 *King Edward I* rounds the sea wall at Teignmouth with the down "Torbay Express" from Bristol to Kingswear. A classic location for a classic locomotive and train.

(Roger Siviter)

Back jacket: Southern Railway King Arthur Class 4-6-0 No 777 *Sir Lamiel* climbs out of Sherborne with the 15.00 Exeter to Salisbury special charter train. 21 June 1992.

(Roger Siviter)

Introduction

It is now almost a quarter of a century since main line steam returned to the South West of England, first of all in 1985 on the GWR line between Bristol and Plymouth, and one trip from Plymouth to Truro in the Duchy of Cornwall. These trips were run as part of the GWR 150th anniversary celebrations, but it would be some nine years later, in 1994, that steam was seen again on the Bristol to Devon route, and 1995 before steam returned to Cornwall, with a trip from Exeter to Penzance (on 14 October of that year) with Britannia Pacific No 70000 *Britannia* in charge on the Cornish leg of the journey.

The former Southern Railway route from Salisbury to Exeter saw the return of main line steam in the autumn of 1986, and then intermittent steam workings right up to the present day.

However, the GWR route now sees regular summer steam workings from Bristol to Kingswear - the "Torbay Express" - as well as over the years (from 1994) many trips to Plymouth, and every now and then trips into Cornwall.

Over the years, a great variety of locomotives have been used on these routes, mainly GWR and SR engines, but as we can see in the book also some LMS, LNER and BR Standard locomotives as well.

Our book is in journey order, starting from Salisbury to Exeter, including a glimpse of the Weymouth line from Yeovil. From Exeter we visit the former SR line to Oakhampton and to Barnstaple, which diverge at Coleford junction, some twelve miles west of Exeter.

Our journey restarts at Cogload junction, just north east of Taunton where the GWR line from Bristol meets the line from Paddington. We then head back to Exeter and on to Plymouth, and then into Cornwall, finishing our journey at Penzance. The following branch lines are also featured:- Paignton, Gunnislake, Par Docks, Fowey and Falmouth.

It has been a pleasure to compile this book. This is in no small measure due to photographers Hugh Ballantyne, Peter Doel and Mark Wilkins for allowing me use of their excellent pictures. I must also thank my wife for typing, etc. and the odd picture or so! Finally, my thanks go to all railwaymen, professional and amateur, who make it all possible.

Roger Siviter, ARPS.
Teignmouth, Devon. 2009.

ISBN 978095411509-8
Price:- £16.99
80 pages, 116 colour pictures + 2 black & white prints.
Size:- 285 mm x 220 mm. 150 gsm gloss paper.

Address:-
Great Bear Publishing,
2, Seacliff,
First Drive,
Dawlish Road,
Teignmouth,
Devon TQ14 8TX
Tel:- 01626 774787

Below: After the unsuccessful trip of 7 April 1985, it would be the end of October 1985 before No 6000 *King George V* appeared in the south-west again.

No 6000 and No 7819 *Hinton Manor* are pictured at Plymouth Laira depot on 27 October 1985, prior to leaving with the final GWR 150 Plymouth to Bristol special train.   (*Christina Siviter*)

Above: We start our south-western journey at Salisbury station on the morning of 2 October 1986. Ex SR Merchant Navy Pacific No 35028 *Clan Line* is seen busy shunting stock before leaving with a crew familiarisation trip to Yeovil Junction and return, prior to the first public special train on the following Sunday (5 October). This crew train would be the first steam on the Salisbury to Exeter line for some 20 years.   *(Roger Siviter)*

Top right: No 35028 *Clan Line* is stabled in Salisbury station (former LSWR) on 2 October 1986 after working the crew familiarisation trip to Yeovil Junction and return. The locomotive had just turned on the triangle to the east of the station.

For part of my army service, from May 1954 to January 1955, I was stationed at Bulford Camp near Salisbury, and over the period of that time I made several rail journeys to and from Birmingham. Often for the return journey half a dozen of us would catch a train from Birmingham Snow Hill station at around 9.00 p.m., which travelled via Oxford and Reading, and arrived in Salisbury between 1.30 a.m. and 2.00 a.m. But that's when the fun started, for at that time of the morning there was only one taxi at the station, usually an Austin Big Six, and the train was full of squaddies. So we had to make sure that the quickest of our party was off the train first, in order to get the taxi for us, otherwise we would have walk about 7 miles back to camp. So you can imagine the scramble it always was!   *((Roger Siviter))*

Bottom right: Some of the special steam workings in October 1986 were also worked by LNER Class A4 Pacific No 4498 *Sir Nigel Gresley* and GWR Modified Hall Class No 6998 *Burton Agnes Hall*, both seen here in bay platform No 5 at Salisbury station on the evening of Saturday 18 October 1986.
       (Mark Wilkins)

Left: Celebrity visitor to the Waterloo - Exeter line on Saturday 20 March 1993 was BR Standard Class 7P6F Pacific No 70000 *Britannia*.

On this bright spring day, the Pacific locomotive approaches Wilton Road bridge as it pulls out of the city of Salisbury with 'The South Western Limited" - the 10.47 Clapham Junction to Yeovil Junction train. In the background is Salisbury Cathedral with its 400 ft high spire.

The Britannia Pacifics were first introduced in 1951, and many of the class could still be seen at work on the West Coast Main Line north of Crewe until the end of 1967. Two examples remain in preservation. Besides No 70000 we also have No 70013 *Oliver Cromwell* which is famous for having worked part of the final BR steam train from Manchester to Carlisle via the Settle & Carlisle route on 11 August 1968 - the "15 Guinea Special".

(*Mark Wilkins*)

Ex LNER Class A4 Pacific *Union of South Africa* crosses over Barford St. Martin viaduct, some six miles west of Salisbury, with a Salisbury to Yeovil train, on a November day in the late 1990s.

The A4 Pacifics were designed by Sir Nigel Gresley and first introduced in 1935. Several examples are preserved, including No 4468 *Mallard*, the holder of the world speed record for steam traction - 126 mph.

(Peter Doel)

Top left: On 2 October 1986, No 35028 is seen returning to Salisbury from Yeovil Junction with the crew familiarisation train. The location is the closed station at Dinton (three miles to the west of Barford St. Martin). Note the LSWR station buildings, etc. and the military sidings on the left and right hand sides to serve the nearby military depots.
(Roger Siviter)

Bottom left: A close-up of GWR Modified Hall Class No 6998 *Burton Agnes Hall* as it heads through Tisbury on 5 October 1986 with the 14.17 Salisbury to Yeovil Junction charter train. The Modified Hall Class were introduced in 1944 and were a development of the original Hall Class, the re-designer being Hawksworth. *(Christina Siviter)*

Above: Clan Line pulls away from Tisbury station on the morning of 2 October 1986 with an outward test run from Salisbury to Yeovil Junction. The SR Merchant Navy Class Pacifics were designed by Bulleid and first introduced in 1941. They were rebuilt in 1956, with Walschaerts valve gear and modified details, and the air smoothed casing removed.
(Roger Siviter)

Top left: On 10 June 1992, another crew familiarisation trip was run, this time from Eastleigh to Exeter and return to Salisbury. In charge was BR Standard Class 4MT No 75069 and ex SR rebuilt West Country Pacific No 34027 *Taw Valley*. The train is seen at West Hatch near Semley on the outward journey, some 17 miles west of Salisbury.   *(Roger Siviter)*

Bottom left: A4 Pacific No 4498 *Sir Nigel Gresley* looks a treat as it approaches Buckhorn Weston tunnel on Sunday 26 October 1986 with the 11.17 Salisbury to Yeovil Junction special train.   *(Peter Doel)*

Above: No 35028 *Clan Line* is pictured leaving Buckhorn Weston tunnel on 2 October 1986 with the return crew training trip from Yeovil Junction to Salisbury. This location is sometimes referred to as Gillingham tunnel, being located some two miles west of the Dorset town.   *(Roger Siviter)*

Above: SR Class S15 4-6-0 No 828 runs past the former SR signal box, which also serves as a ticket office, at Templecombe station with the 10.55 Yeovil Junction to Eastleigh special train, on 10 October 1994. Templecombe was originally Templecombe Junction, which connected the Waterloo - Exeter line to the Somerset & Dorset Joint Railway. The S & D line sadly closed in March 1966, and Templecombe station itself closed a few weeks later, in May 1966. It reopened in 1982, and a new station building was completed in 1988, all with considerable support from the local community's railway action group.   (*Hugh Ballantyne*)

Below: 4-6-0 No 777 SR King Arthur Class *Sir Lamiel* climbs the 1 in 100 incline at mile-post 113 1/2 near Stowell on the double track section between Templecombe and Yeovil Junction. The train is an Andover to Exeter special charter. 28 June 1992.
(*Hugh Ballantyne*)

Above: At the same location as the previous picture, only this time on the down line, ex SR West Country 4-6-2 No 34027 *Taw Valley* has steam to spare as it approaches the summit of the 1 in 100 bank with a special train from Andover to Exeter on 21 June 1992.

(Roger Siviter)

Below No 828 again, this time passing Stowell with the 10.55 Yeovil Junction to Eastleigh, also on 10 October 1994. The S15 Class 4-6-0s were first introduced in 1920 on the LSWR, and were designed by Urie. However, No 828 was one of a batch introduced in 1927 to a modified design by Maunsell. They were primarily mixed traffic locomotives.

(Hugh Ballantyne)

Left: BR Standard Class 4MT 4-6-0 No 75069 climbs the 1 in 80 of Sherborne bank, and approaches Milborne Port with the 15.00 Exeter to Salisbury steam special on Sunday 28 June 1992.

This design was first introduced in 1951, but No 75069 was built at Swindon in 1955. From 1957 onwards, it was fitted with a double blastpipe and chimney. Like many locomotives, it was rescued from Woodham's scrapyard at Barry and restored on the Severn Valley Railway. Several examples of the class have been preserved. *(Roger Siviter)*

Below: This side view of No 777 *Sir Lamiel* shows up well the elegance of the King Arthur Class 4-6-0 (N15) which was introduced on the Southern Railway in 1925, and designed by R.E.L.Maunsell. The location is the foot of Sherborne bank, and the train is the 15.00 Exeter to Salisbury steam special. 21 June 1992. *(Roger Siviter)*

Sherborne Castle provides the backdrop as Nos 75069 and 34027 tackle the three miles of Sherborne bank with the return crew training trip from Exeter to Salisbury on 10 June 1992.

(Roger Siviter)

Above: On 9 October 1994, Class M7 0-4-4T No 30129 leaves Yeovil Pen Mill station with a shuttle train to Yeovil Junction. On the right hand side is Class S15 4-6-0 No 828 which is due to take out a special train to Eastleigh from Yeovil Junction on the following day. Pen Mill station is on the former GWR line from Castle Cary to Weymouth. *(Hugh Ballantyne)*

Below: On the same day, No 30129 makes a fine sight climbing to Evershot tunnel en route from Yeovil Junction to Maiden Newton on the Weymouth line. *(Hugh Ballantyne)*

Above: GWR King Class 4-6-0 No 6024 *King Edward I* climbs the 1 in 50 bank at Upwey with a return Weymouth to Didcot special charter train, the "Hardy Flyer". In the background is the famous Dorset resort of Weymouth, which will be home to the 2012 Olympic sailing events. 5 September 1998.   *(Roger Siviter)*

Below: Our final picture of the Class M7 0-4-4T (taken on 9 October 1994) shows No 30129 pulling away from Yeovil Junction's home signals and approaching the junction station with an afternoon shuttle train from Yeovil Pen Mill station. These handsome Drummond 0-4-4T locomotives were first introduced on the LSWR in 1897. No 30129 was one of a batch fitted for push-and-pull working.   *(Hugh Ballantyne)*

Top left: SR Class S15 4-6-0 looks a fine sight as it pulls out of Yeovil Junction station on 10 October 1994 with a special train bound for Eastleigh. (See also pictures on pages 12 and 13.)   *(Hugh Ballantyne)*

Bottom left: King Edward I runs through Yeovil Junction station before being serviced and turned, and then running light down to Weymouth to take out the "Hardy Flyer". 5 September 1998. (See picture on previous page.)   *(Roger Siviter)*

Above: Yeovil Junction still boasts a turntable, which is ideal for steam special trains. These next two pictures show first No 35028 *Clan Line* being turned on 20 October 1986 after running in from Salisbury; the second scene shows King Arthur Class 4-6-0 *Sir Lamiel* being turned on 21 June 1992. No.35028 was purchased in working order from BR by the Merchant Navy Locomotive Preservation Society. No. 777 was restored to main line running condition in 1982 by the Humberside Locomotive Preservation Group. The turntable and adjacent building are all part of the Yeovil Railway Centre.   *(Two pictures: Roger Siviter)*

Above: This final scene at Yeovil Junction station shows West Country Pacific No 34027 *Taw Valley* leaving with a special charter train to Exeter on 21 June 1992. This class of locomotive, designed by Bullied, was first introduced on the SR in 1945, complete with air smoothed casing. This was removed from No 34027 in 1957 and also rebuilt with Walschaerts valve gear. No 34027 was rescued from Barry scrapyard in 1980, and restored on the Severn Valley Railway in 1987. (*Hugh Ballantyne*)

Below: Looking like a two-coach local train, especially with the single track and tender-first working, but in actual fact a locomotive and stock movement train from Salisbury to Exeter, to enable BR Standard Class 4MT 4-6-0 No 75069 to work back on the 15.00 Exeter - Salisbury charter train seen on page 15. The location is North Perrott, some two miles east of the Somerset town of Crewkerne. 28 June 1992. (*Roger Siviter*)

Above: On 21 June 1992, 4-6-0 *Sir Lamiel* heads east out of Crewkerne, and runs through the rich-looking farming land near North Perrott with the 15.00 Exeter to Salisbury steam special.

(Roger Siviter)

Below: Seaton Junction, once the junction for the branch line to the Devon seaside resort of Seaton, is the setting as 4-6-0

No 75069 and 4-6-2 No 34027 *Taw Valley* run through the remains of the station with the return crew working train from Exeter to Salisbury, on 10 June 1992.

This station and the branch line closed in 1966. However, part of the old trackbed of the branch line from Seaton to Colyford now forms the popular 2ft 9in gauge Seaton Tramway. *(Roger Siviter)*

After Seaton Junction station, the line climbs for around five miles at 1 in 80 westwards towards the town of Honiton. The first scene (opposite, top) shows No 75069 as it descends Honiton bank and approaches Seaton Junction station on 28 June 1992 with the 15.00 Exeter to Salisbury train.
(Roger Siviter)

The second scene (above) shows LNER Class A3 Pacific No 4472 *Flying Scotsman* climbing Honiton bank on Wednesday 29 December 1999 with the 11.40 Yeovil Pen Mill to Exeter special charter train. No 4472, probably the most famous locomotive in the world, was designed by Gresley and built at the LNER Doncaster works in 1923.
(Mark Wilkins)

Opposite, bottom: A rare visitor to the South West was BR Standard Class 5MT 4-6-0 No 73096, seen here approaching Exeter St James station on 15 March 2003 with a Waterloo - Exeter charter train. No 73096 was built at Derby in 1955 and withdrawn from service in 1967. It was rescued from Barry scrapyard in 1985 and restored at Ropley on the Mid-Hants Railway.
(Roger Siviter)

Ex Southern Railway West Country Pacific No 34027 *Taw Valley* gives off a fine exhaust as it leaves Exeter Central station and begins the 1 in 100 climb up to Exmouth junction on Sunday morning 19 September 1993. The special train is the "Sarum Limited", the 09.56 Exeter to Salisbury.

On the right hand side, the old Exeter signal box is still in situ, but has been out of use since the area was re-signalled in 1985. Also in this picture, at the front and rear of the signal box are the tracks leading to the small goods yard adjacent to Exeter Central station which served the cement depot. The signal box has now been demolished and blocks of flats have replaced the cement depot. *(Mark Wilkins)*

Left: In 2008, some 40 years after working the final BR steam train - the "15 Guinea Special" - Britannia Pacific No 70013 *Oliver Cromwell* returned to main line steam duty and worked on several special charter trains in the second half of the year, including a Waterloo to Exeter train, seen here approaching Exeter Central station on 14 September 2008. *(Roger Siviter)*

Top: Another rare visitor to the Salisbury - Exeter line was SR Lord Nelson Class 4-6-0 No 850 *Lord Nelson*, seen here coming into St Davids station, at the foot of the 1 in 37 bank between Exeter Central and Exeter St Davids station with a train from Waterloo. 8 July 2007. *(Roger Siviter)*

Bottom: Our next location is Cowley Bridge junction, just over a mile north of Exeter St Davids station, where the former SR line to Plymouth (now only to Oakhampton / Meldon Quarry, and the former branch line to Barnstaple) leaves the ex GWR line to Paddington.

On the afternoon of 1 May 1994, BR Standard 4MT 2-6-4T No 80079 is seen at the rear of a Barnstaple to Exeter special charter train, just leaving the former SR line at Cowley Bridge junction. The train locomotive is 2-6-4 No 80080. On the right is the Cowley Bridge Inn. *(Roger Siviter)*

Above: On 25 October 1997, GWR Class 4300 2-6-0 No 7325 and LMS Class 5MT 2-6-0 No 2968 disturb the peace at Yeoford station as they run through with an Exeter - Oakhampton - Meldon Quarry special train. The track on the left hand side is to Barnstaple, the lines separating at Coleford junction, just west of Yeoford. *(Roger Siviter)*

Below: 2-6-4T No 80080 hurries through Lapford on the Barnstaple line with the 16.10 Barnstaple to Exeter charter train on 1 May 1994. Out of sight, No 80079 is at the rear of the train. *(Hugh Ballantyne)*

Above: The "Mighty Moguls" 2-6-0s Nos 2968 and 7325, as they are affectionately known, are caught by the camera as they speed through Cogload junction with a Bristol - Exeter - Oakhampton special on 25 October 1997. (See picture opposite, upper). LMS 2-6-0 No 2968 was designed by Stanier and introduced in 1933. The GWR 2-6-0 No 7325 was introduced in 1932, and was a modified design by Collett, based on a Churchward design of 1911.

(Roger Siviter)

Below: On the evening of 15 May 1999, ex LNER Class V2 2-6-2 No 60800 *Green Arrow* approaches Cogload junction with a return Par - Reading special charter train, the motive power for the outward working being preserved Deltic Class diesel No D9000 *Royal Scots Grey*. In BR steam days, Cogload water troughs were situated just west of this location.

(Roger Siviter)

Above: Two miles east of Taunton is Creech St. Michael, where our next picture was taken on 28 August 2005. The train is the "Torbay Express" from Bristol to Kingswear, hauled by GWR King Class 4-6-0 No 6024 *King Edward I* . Until 1986, the line from Taunton to Cogload junction was four tracks, as is evident in this picture. *(Roger Siviter)*

Opposite page: These two pictures, taken in 1985, show well the eastern side of Taunton station, prior to the re-signalling of the area in 1986.

The first scene, taken on 14 July, shows the Newton Abbot to Bristol "GWR 150" special train as it heads away from Taunton, hauled by GWR Castle Class 4-6-0 No 5051 *Drysllwyn Castle* and GWR Hall Class 4-6-0 No 4930 *Hagley Hall*. Completing the picture is a fine array of GWR bracket signals.

Turning round from the previous picture but this time on 15 September 1985, and we see No 5051 again, only this time with Castle Class 4-6-0 No 7029 *Clun Castle*, as they leave Taunton and head for Bristol with the "Great Western Limited" from Plymouth. At the rear of the train is Taunton East signal box, behind which runs the Taunton goods relief line. *(Two pictures: Christina Siviter)*

Above: GWR Manor Class 4-6-0 No 7802 *Bradley Manor* leaves Taunton station and heads for Minehead - terminus of the West Somerset Railway - with a special charter train from Hereford via Bristol. The line to Minehead leaves the Exeter line at Norton Fitzwarren, some two miles west of this location.

The BR Minehead branch line closed in January 1971, but that year the new West Somerset Railway was formed and in 1976 trains ran between Minehead and Blue Anchor, and by 1979 to Bishop's Lydeard, from where there is still obviously a connection to the BR Taunton - Exeter route. 10 March 2007. *(Roger Siviter)*

Opposite page, top: A fine sight as BR Standard Class 4MT 2-6-4T locomotives Nos 80080 and 80079 emerge from Whiteball tunnel and into the county of Devon with a Bristol to Exeter steam special on 1 May 1994.

These sturdy looking tank locomotives were first introduced in 1951, and Nos 80079 and 80080 were built in 1954, and were withdrawn in 1965. Both locomotives were rescued from Barry scrapyard, No 80079 being restored on the Severn Valley Railway and No 80080 by the Peak Railway Society. *(Hugh Ballantyne)*

Opposite page, bottom: Veteran GWR City Class 4-4-0 No 3440 *City of Truro* hurries down Whiteball bank with the "100 Ocean Mail" steam special from Bristol to Kingswear on 8 May 2004. This train, and the return journey on 10 May, was run to commemorate the centenary of the occasion on 9 May 1904 when *City of Truro* reached 102.3 mph on Wellington bank with a Plymouth to Paddington "Ocean Mail Special". At the time, this was the highest speed recorded by a train. *(Roger Siviter)*

Above: Up trains on Whiteball bank face a steep climb of nearly five miles from just north of Tiverton Junction up to the summit in Whiteball tunnel, including the final two miles at 1 in 115. However, on 14 July 1985, GWR Castle No 5051 and Hall No 4930 are seen climbing up to Whiteball summit in fine style with the "Great Western Limited" from Newton Abbot to Bristol.

The Castle Class 4-6-0s were introduced on the GWR in 1923, and the 4-6-0 Hall Class in 1928. Both were designed by C. B. Collett. No 5051 was rescued from Barry scrapyard and preserved by the Great Western Society at Didcot. No 4930 was also a Barry scrapyard engine and preserved on the Severn Valley Railway. *(Hugh Ballantyne)*

Opposite page, top: The two Castle 4-6-0s No 7029 *Clun Castle* (built in 1950) and No 5051 *Drysllwyn Castle* make a fine sight as they speed through Tiverton Junction on 8 September 1985 with the "Great Western Limited" from Plymouth to Bristol. To complete the scene is a fine array of GWR signals. *(Christina Siviter)*

Opposite page, bottom: On 5 April 1997, the setting sun just illuminates No 6024 *King Edward I* as it hurries through the remains of Cullompton station with a return Plymouth to Taunton steam special. On the left is the old GWR goods shed, now long gone, and in its place is part of a garage and M5 service cafe. The station itself closed in 1964. *(Roger Siviter)*

The unique Class 8P BR Pacific No 71000 *Duke of Gloucester* heads through Rewe, some five miles north east of Exeter in the Exe Valley, with a Plymouth to Bristol charter train, the "Devonian Duke". This picture was taken on the evening of 28 May 2007.

No 71000 (the only member of its class) had a short life on BR, being built in 1954, and then withdrawn from service in 1962. After many years, first at Crewe and then at Barry waiting to be scrapped, it was purchased by the Duke of Gloucester Steam Locomotive Trust, and restored at the Great Central Railway at Loughborough.

(Roger Siviter)

A lovely sight at Cowley Bridge junction on the afternoon of 16 March 2002, as a pair of GWR Hall Class 4-6-0s head for Exeter St Davids station and on to Kingswear with an excursion from Gloucester - "The Torbay Limited". The locomotives are No 4965 *Rood Ashton Hall* and No 4936 *Kinlet Hall*, both preserved at Tyseley Museum. Note also the tender sizes, No 4965 with the smaller 3500 gallon tender and No 4936 with the 4000 gallon tender.

These Class 5 mixed traffic locomotives were generally regarded as the GWR "maids of all work" engines. Both these locomotives were built at Swindon in 1929.

(Roger Siviter)

Above: On 16 March 1996, GWR Manor Class 4-6-0 No 7802 approaches Cowley Bridge junction from Exeter St Davids station with a Totnes to Worcester special charter train.

Introduced in 1938, these lightweight 4-6-0 locomotives were designed by C. B. Collett, mainly for use on secondary lines. No 7802 was rescued from Barry by the Earlstoke Manor Fund and restored on the Severn Valley Railway. *(Roger Siviter)*

Opposite page, top: SR Lord Nelson Class 7P 4-6-0 No 850 *Lord Nelson* runs into Exeter St Davids station on 8 July 2007 with a special train from Waterloo. (See also picture on page 27, upper).

This class of locomotive was designed for the Southern Railway by R. E. L. Maunsell and first introduced in 1926. They were modified by Bulleid in 1938 with multiple-jet blastpipe, large diameter chimney and redesigned cylinders and tender. They were all withdrawn from service by 1962, and No 850 was preserved as part of the National Collection. It was originally restored to main line running condition at Steamtown, Carnforth, in 1980. *(Christina Siviter)*

Opposite page, bottom: Passing by the old GWR signal box at the site of Exminster station on 30 November 1996 is the unusual combination of GWR King Class 4-6-0 No 6024 *King Edward I* and GWR Class 4300 2-6-0 No 7325 in charge of a Plymouth to Worcester special - "The Devonian". *(Roger Siviter)*

A delightful picture taken from the hillside at Powderham, and showing ex-LMS Class 5MT 4-6-0 No 45407 *The Lancashire Fusilier* and a rake of maroon stock heading for Exeter on the evening of 12 August 2002 with a special train from Paignton to Exeter - "The Dawlish Donkey". Just beyond the train is the Exeter Canal and then the River Exe, beyond which is the riverside town of Topsham. Completing the scene are the rolling hills of South East Devon.

(Peter Doel)

Above: "The Penzance Castles" special of 4 May 2002 from Bristol to Penzance was hauled by GWR Castle Class 4-6-0s No 5029 *Nunney Castle* and No 5051 *Drysllwyn Castle*. The special is seen speeding along the Exe Estuary at Starcross as it heads for Plymouth and Penzance that sunny spring day. *(Peter Doel)*

Below: Until the advent of metal fencing in 2007, one of the most popular and picturesque locations for photographers on the sea wall area between Starcross and Teignmouth was Cockwood Harbour. On 14 July 1985 GWR 4-6-0s No 5051 *Drysllwyn Castle* and No 4930 *Hagley Hall* make a fine sight as they head across the causeway at Cockwood with a Newton Abbot to Bristol "GWR 150" special. *(Christina Siviter)*

Above: Another picture at Cockwood, this time from the other end of the harbour, showing GWR Class 14XX 0-4-2T No 1450 on 12 April 1998 with the 17.22 Exeter St Davids to Newton Abbot shuttle train - "The Dawlish Donkey". *(Hugh Ballantyne)*

Below: "The Devonian" from Bristol to Plymouth leaves Dawlish Warren and approaches Langstone Rock at it heads for Newton Abbot and Plymouth on 21 August 2004. In charge are GWR Castle Class 4-6-0s No 5029 *Nunney Castle* and No 5051 *Drysllwyn Castle*. *(Roger Siviter)*

Above: The first shuttle train of the day from Exeter St Davids to Newton Abbot nears Langstone Rock on 12 April 1998 with GWR 0-4-2T No 1450 in charge.

These 0-4-2T locomotives were first introduced in 1932 and designed by C. B. Collett. They were used mainly on light branch work, and push-and-pull working. No 1450 was preserved originally by the Dart Valley Railway at Buckfastleigh. *(Hugh Ballantyne)*

Top right: This picture was taken from the top of Langstone Rock on 1 September 1985, and shows GWR Castle Class 4-6-0s Nos 5051 and 7029 with the "Great Western Limited" from Plymouth to Bristol. *(Christina Siviter)*

Bottom right: On 5 September 2004, 4-6-0 No 5051 *Drysllwyn Castle* runs past the Rockstone and nears Dawlish with a Bristol to Kingswear train. At the rear of the picture on the right hand side can be seen Langstone Rock, from where the previous picture was taken. *(Roger Siviter)*

Left: A winter's day at Dawlish as GWR City Class 4-4-0 No 3440 *City of Truro* passes the Rockstone cliffs with a Plymouth to Bristol special on 3 December 2004. This famous GWR locomotive was designed by Churchward and built at Swindon in 1903, and taken out of service in 1931, and was then presented to the Railway Museum at York to be part of the National Collection. Over the years, it has made many returns to main line and preserved line running.
(Roger Siviter)

Right: The "Torbay Express"" of 6 July 2008 was hauled by ex SR unrebuilt Battle of Britain Pacific No 34067 *Tangmere*, seen here approaching Dawlish station with the return working from Kingswear to Bristol. These locomotives were first introduced in 1946, and designed by O. V. Bulleid. In 1957, several members of the class were rebuilt and their air-smoothed casing was removed. These locomotives were not uncommon along the seawall in BR steam days. I remember "copping" one at Dawlish Warren station during a summer holiday in 1951!
(Roger Siviter)

Below: GWR King Class 4-6-0 No 6024 *King Edward I* runs round the sea wall at Dawlish with the down "Torbay Express" from Bristol to Kingswear on 8 July 2007. The King Class was designed by Collett and first introduced in 1927. No 6024 was built in 1930 and withdrawn from service in June 1962. It was rescued from Barry scrapyard by the 6024 Preservation Society, and restored at Quainton Road. It returned to main line service in 1990.
(Roger Siviter)

BR Standard Class 4MT 2-6-4T locomotives Nos 80080 and 80079 make a fine sight as they hurry round the sea wall at Dawlish with the 12.47 Exeter to Paignton charter train on 2 May 1994. In the background on the right hand side can be seen the GWR station at Dawlish and also the GWR signal box, situated on the end of the up platform. *(Hugh Ballantyne)*

48

GWR 4-6-0 No 5051 and No 4930 are caught by the camera as they head through Horse Cove with the down "Great Western Limited" on 7 July 1985. This location, also known as Shell Cove, is situated between the South Devon seaside resorts of Dawlish (seen in the background) and Teignmouth.

(Peter Doel)

Left: Our next location is almost a mile south of the previous picture, and is the Parson & Clerk tunnel. On 28 May 2005, BR Standard Class 8P 4-6-2 No 71000 *Duke of Gloucester* makes a splendid sight as it bursts out of the tunnel with the "Devonian Duke" from Bristol to Plymouth. (See also picture on page 36). *(Christina Siviter)*

Above: It is a rare occasion when you get an up morning steam special on the sea wall. However, one such occasion was on 15 February 2003 when GWR Castle Class 4-6-0 No 5029 *Nunney Castle* was in charge of a Newton Abbot - Bristol - Swansea special charter train - "The Exe - Tawe". The special is seen in beautiful winter sunshine as it runs along the sea wall at Teignmouth and heads towards the Parson & Clerk tunnel. *(Mark Wilkins)*

Above: On Sunday 20 July 2008, No 6024 *King Edward I* approaches Sprey Point near Teignmouth with the down "Torbay Express" from Bristol to Kingswear. On the extreme right hand side of the picture can be seen the entrance to the Parson & Clerk tunnel.

(Roger Siviter)

Opposite top: Another royal visitor to the sea wall, only this time from the LMS. Class 8P Princess Class Pacific No 6201 *Princess Elizabeth* runs along the sea wall towards Teignmouth with a charter train from Taunton to Plymouth on a sunny 7 October 2006. On the right hand side is Sprey Point. These handsome locomotives were designed by Stanier and introduced in 1933.

(Christina Siviter)

Opposite bottom: Shaldon Bridge, Teignmouth, is the location as the down "Torbay Express", hauled by *King Edward I*, heads for Newton Abbot and Kingswear on Sunday 5 August 2005.

(Roger Siviter)

Above left: Turning round from the previous picture, and we see BR Standard Class 4MT 2-6-0 No 76079 (popularly known as the "Pocket Rocket") nearing Shaldon Bridge with the 11.32 Paignton - Exeter charter train - "The Dawlish Donkey" - on 16 August 2001. These BR mixed traffic Mogul locomotives were first introduced in 1952, No 76079 being built at Horwich in 1957. It was one of the last members of the class to be withdrawn, in December 1967. It was rescued from Barry scrapyard by Steamport, Southport.
(Roger Siviter)

Bottom left: A GWR Hall 4-6-0 and Manor 4-6-0 make a grand sight as they head down the Teign estuary near Bishopsteignton with the first main line steam working out of Plymouth for over twenty years - the "Great Western Limited" to Bristol. The date is the 8 April 1985 and the locomotives are No 4930 *Hagley Hall* and No 7819 *Hinton Manor*, both Severn Valley locomotives.
(Peter Doel)

Above: Another GWR 150 anniversary scene from 1985, this time on 7 July 1985, with GWR 4-6-0 Nos 5051 and 4930 departing from Newton Abbot station with the down "Great Western Limited" to Plymouth. Within two years, due to re-signalling in the area, scenes like this would drastically change. *(Christina Siviter)*

Above: On a clear crisp November day (Saturday 13th) in 2004, *King Edward I* climbs up to Aller junction with "The Devonian" from Bristol to Plymouth. Although still popularly referred to as "Aller junction", with the re-signalling of 1987 this is now a divergence of the Plymouth and Paignton lines.

(Roger Siviter)

Above right: A rare visitor to this area is GWR Class 5700 0-6-0 pannier tank No 9600 seen climbing up to Aller with the 15.28 Newton Abbot to Paignton shuttle train on 13 May 2000 - "The Newton Antelope".

These Collett designed tank locomotives were first introduced in 1929 for shunting and light goods work. Note the livery of the coaching stock - BR "plum and spilt milk", dating back to the early BR days.

(Roger Siviter)

Bottom right: This final view at Aller, taken on 17 August 2003, clearly shows the divergence of the Plymouth and Paignton lines. GWR 4-6-0 No 5051 *Earl Bathurst* approaches Aller with a Kingswear / Paignton to Bristol charter train. The line to Plymouth can be seen swinging away on the right hand side, which is also the start of the notorious Dainton bank. The site of Aller junction signal box can be seen above the fourth and fifth coaches.

(Roger Siviter)

Left: The up "Torbay Express" from Kingswear to Bristol, with GWR 4-6-0 *King Edward I* in charge, climbs the 1 in 73 out of Torre (on the Paignton branch) and approaches Kingkerswell on Sunday 27 July 2008. From Paignton to Kingswear the line is privately owned by the Paignton & Dartmouth Railway.
(Roger Siviter)

Above: We are now back on the main line to Plymouth. The location is Stoneycombe, roughly half way up the notorious Dainton bank. For down trains, this means a climb of around 1 in 36 at its steepest.

On Saturday 27 October 2001, one of Sir William Stanier's handsome LMS Coronation Class Pacifics, No 6233 *Duchess of Sutherland* climbs the very steep grade at Stoneycombe with a Bristol to Plymouth special charter train - "The Mayflower".

These classic locomotives were first introduced in 1937 and, together with the Princess Coronation Class Pacifics, saw service on the Paddington - Plymouth line in the 1950s, when the King Class locomotives were withdrawn from service for a short period. *(Mark Wilkins)*

Left: The down "Great Western Limited" of 7 July 1985 (seen leaving Newton Abbot on page 55) stalled on Dainton bank and the train terminated at Totnes with assistance from Class 50 diesel No 50045 *Achilles*.

No 5051 and No 4930 seem to be in no trouble at all as they climb Dainton on that fateful day. But to quote the photographer, no sooner had they passed him than they came to rest. After that, BR would only allow the remaining steam specials of 1985 to start from Plymouth and run in the up direction.

(Mark Wilkins)

Below: A wonderful show of exhaust as GWR City Class 4-4-0 No 3440 *City of Truro* storms up Dainton bank on 27 November 2004 with a Bristol to Plymouth special charter train. This location is just short of the summit near Dainton tunnel.

(Peter Doel)

Opposite page: After failing at Taunton on 7 April 1985, it would be the end of October that year before GWR King Class 4-6-0 No 6000 *King George V* next appeared in the South West. This was for the final GWR 150 "Great Western Limited" from Plymouth to Bristol, on 27 October 1985. And sadly this was No 6000's one and only trip in the area, for in 1987 *King George V* was taken out of service, and there were to be no more steam specials in Devon until 1994.

The first picture shows No 6000 and Manor Class 4-6-0 No 7819 *Hinton Manor* leaving Plymouth Laira, depot for Plymouth North Road station, for the final up "Great Western Limited" of 1985. In the next picture we see the pair tackling the climb of Dainton bank from the west on that final Sunday. (See also picture on page 3.)

(Two pictures: Roger Siviter)

Above: On 31 March 2007, No 6024 *King Edward I* and No 5051 *Drysllwyn Castle* speed through Totnes station (at the foot of Dainton bank) and start the nine mile climb of Rattery bank with grades as steep as 1 in 46 in places. The special train is "The Cornishman" from Bristol to Penzance. Note the creamery chimney on the left hand side. The creamery has now closed but the chimney remains in situ.

(Roger Siviter)

Above: A pair of GWR Castle Class locomotives No 7029 *Clun Castle* and No 5051 *Drysllwyn Castle* descend the lower slopes of Rattery bank and approach Totnes station with the "Great Western Limited" from Plymouth to Bristol on 8 September 1985. This view gives some idea of the steepness of the incline which in steam days neccessitated the use of banking locomotives at Totnes.

(Christina Siviter)

Bottom right: Brent station, once the junction for the Kingsbridge branch, is our next location as on 15 September 1999 ex LNER Class V2 2-6-2 No 60800 *Green Arrow* runs through the site of the station with "The Eastern Envoy" from Par to Reading. The Kingsbridge branch closed in 1963, and Brent station in 1964, but the old signal box remains as a tool store, etc. The LNER V2 locomotives were designed by Sir Nigel Gresley and first introduced in 1936. In the background are the fringes of Dartmoor.

(Roger Siviter)

Above: The first steam working into Cornwall since 1985 occurred on 14 October 1995, with a train from Exeter to Penzance. The first section to Plymouth, seen here leaving Totnes, was hauled by Manor Class No 7802 *Bradley Manor* and BR Britannia Class Pacific No 70000 *Britannia*, the Pacific then taking the train "The Duchy Explorer" from Plymouth to Penzance. *(Roger Siviter)*

Above: The train seen on page 63 returned on the 7 April 2007, only this time as the first leg, from Penzance to Bristol, of the "Great Britain" special which ran over the following week to the north of Scotland behind steam power and via many routes. The 7 April special with No 6024 and No 5051 in charge heads over Blachford viaduct at Cornwood, near Ivybridge, with the first leg of the "Great Britain" special. *(Roger Siviter)*

Below: After its special trip to Truro on 6 September 1985 (the first steam on the Cornish main line for over twenty years) No 7029 *Clun Castle* brings the empty coaching stock around the curve from Lipson junction to Mount Gould junction adjacent to Plymouth Laira Depot. *(Hugh Ballantyne)*

Above: In March 2007, Ex LMS "Black Five" 4-6-0 No 45407 ran a series of special trains in Devon and Cornwall, including a trip on the Plymouth to Bere Alston branch. This branch was originally part of the Southern main line to Exeter, the section between Bere Alston and Meldon Junction closing in 1968. Bere Alston is also the junction station for the Gunnislake branch, with trains reversing at Bere Alston. No 45407 is seen crossing the River Tavy (a tributary of the Tamar) at Tavy bridge, just over a mile south of Bere Ferrers, with a Bere Alston to Plymouth special charter. 27 March 2007. *(Peter Doel)*

Below: Crossing the Royal Albert Bridge into Devon on 6 May 2002 is GWR 4-6-0 No 5051 plus Class 50 diesel locomotive No 50031 *Hood* as a replacement for GWR 4-6-0 No 5029 *Nunney Castle*. The train is a Penzance to Bristol charter. Above No 5051 can be seen Coombe viaduct, Saltash; also note, below the bridge, the house painted as a Union Jack. *(Roger Siviter)*

Above: BR Standard Class 4MT No 76029 crosses into Cornwall and approaches Saltash station with the 18.00 Plymouth to Parkandillack special train ("Isambard Kingdom Brunel") on 30 May 2006. Dominating the background is Brunel's masterpiece, the Royal Albert Bridge.

(Roger Siviter)

Top right: Forder viaduct, some two miles west of Saltash, is our next location. "Black Five" 4-6-0 No 45407 crosses this handsome viaduct with a Plymouth to St Blazey special on 26 March 2007. Prominent in the background is Trematon Castle. *(Peter Doel)*

Bottom right: Around three miles west of Forder viaduct is the eight-arch Lynher viaduct. On 7 April 2007, the first leg of the "Great Britain" special from Penzance to Bristol, crosses this impressive viaduct with 4-6-0s Nos 6024 and 5051 in charge. *(Christina Siviter)*

Above: The unusual combination of SR Battle of Britain Pacific No 34067 *Tangmere* and GWR King Class 4-6-0 No 6024 *King Edward I* are seen climbing out of Liskeard and crossing the short Bolitho viaduct with "The Eden Limited" from Par to Bristol on the late afternoon of 24 August 2007. The semaphore signal on the left hand side is the first semaphore still in use out of Paddington on the Penzance route. *(Christina Siviter)*

Below: On a bright I February 2003, GWR Castle Class No 5029 *Nunney Castle* runs across Liskeard viaduct and heads for Penzance with a special train from Bristol. *(Peter Doel)*

Above: Lostwithiel is the setting as ex LMS Class 5MT 4-6-0 No 45407 runs down grade into the station with an empty coaching stock special from St Blazey to Plymouth, on Monday 26 March 2007. Dominating the scene is a fine example of a GWR bracket signal.

(Roger Siviter)

Below: Down trains heading out of Lostwithiel station face a steep two mile climb up to Treverrin tunnel. GWR 4-6-0 No 7029 *Clun Castle* and a nice rake of chocolate & cream carriages start the climb away from Lostwithiel on 6 September 1985 with a Plymouth to Truro excursion. Note the tented clay wagons on the right hand side.

(Mark Wilkins)

The freight-only line from Lostwithiel to Carne Point (Fowey) saw steam activity for the first time in many years, when a special excursion from Plymouth down the Fowey branch was run on the 29 May 2006, with BR 2-6-0 No 76079 and Class 37 diesel No D6990 (37411) in charge. The special train is seen in the picturesque setting of Golant Harbour as it heads for Carne Point, with the River Fowey dominating the background. *(Roger Siviter)*

*Top left:*No 76079 again, this time at the rear of the special train seen in the previous picture, on its return journey from Carne Point to Lostwithiel and on to Plymouth. The location is the causeway at Golant. 29 May 2006. *(Roger Siviter)*

*Bottom left:*The famous "Black Five" 4-6-0s of the LMS were designed by Sir William Stanier and were first introduced in 1934. Following the end of steam in August 1968, many examples were preserved, including No 45407, which was later named *The Lancashire Fusilier*. No 45407 is seen here pausing at Par station on Sunday 25 March 2007 with a

special train from Penzance. This station is the junction for St Blazey and the Newquay branch, which can be seen on the right hand side of the picture. *(Christina Siviter)*

*Above:*The following day (26 March 2007) and we see No 45407, this time on a charter train from Plymouth to Par Docks branch, one of the many specials run by "Past Time Rail" during that week. This special is seen on the docks branch, where the Plymouth to Penzance line crosses over it. At the rear of the train is Class 37 No 37410 and at the back of the picture is the English China Clay (ECC) works. *(Roger Siviter)*

Above: On 6 September 1985, No 7029 *Clun Castle* is seen at St Blazey round house for servicing and turning before going on to Truro (tender first) with the special from Plymouth, from where it would return to Plymouth later that afternoon.
(*Hugh Ballantyne*)

Top right: Class 4-6-0s No 5029 and No 5051 climb the 1 in 84 over St Austell viaduct on 4 May 2002, and head west with "The Penzance Castles" special from Taunton to Penzance.
(*Peter Doel*)

Below right: BR Britannia Pacific No 70000 *Britannia* (assisted by Class 47 diesel No 47519) runs through Burngullow on 21 October 1995 with the "Cornubian" from Penzance to Bristol. On the right hand side is the (now) freight-only line to Parkandillack, which originally ran to St Dennis Junction on the Par to Newquay line. Note the main line to Truro is single here - it was singled in 1986, but then doubled again in 2004.
(*Roger Siviter*)

Above: Clun Castle with a Truro to Plymouth special runs across the nine-arch viaduct at Coombe St. Stephen between Truro and St. Austell. The remaining stone piers of Brunel's original timber viaduct can be seen on the left hand side. 6 September 1985.
(Hugh Ballantyne)

Below: Steam specials are fairly rare into Cornwall, and even more so on the Truro to Falmouth branch. On Sunday 20 September 1998, No 6024 *King Edward I* crosses over the Penryn viaduct, some three miles out of Falmouth, with the 16.30 Falmouth to Gloucester charter train - "The Falmouth Packet". *(Mark Wilkins)*

Above: The first leg from Penzance to Bristol of the "Great Britain" special crosses Hayle viaduct on 7 April 2007 with No 6024 and No 5051 in charge. In the background is St. Ives Bay and the Atlantic Ocean. At this point, the county of Cornwall is very narrow, there being no more than five miles between Marazion (on Mount's Bay) and Hayle. *(Peter Doel)*

Below: This picture was taken at Marazion, home of the Pullman camping coaches seen on the left hand side. The date is 21 October 1995, and the train is the "Cornubian" from Penzance to Bristol, hauled by Britannia Pacific No 70000 *Britannia* with assistance from Class 47 diesel No 47519. Above the camping coaches can be seen Mount's Bay and the outskirts of Penzance. *(Mark Wilkins)*

The final two pictures in our South Western journey show GWR King Class 4-6-0 No 6024 *King Edward I* as it approaches and enters Penzance station on 19 September 1998 with a special train from Exeter - "The Penzance Pirate". Because of weight restrictions in GWR / BR days, this was said to be the first visit of the powerful King Class locomotive into Cornwall. The crowds turned out for this historic occasion and the weather remained very fine indeed.

(Two pictures: Roger Siviter)